CREMATION
IS IT CHRISTIAN?

James W. Fraser

LOIZEAUX BROTHERS

Neptune, New Jersey

Revised Edition, July 1985

PRINTED IN THE UNTIED STATES OF AMERICA

CONTENTS

PREFACE

Chapter one of this booklet first appeared in print as a copy of a radio sermon given by the author in Montreal, Canada. Later it was carried by the *Sunday School Times* of the United States and is included in this pamphlet with the *Times'* permission.

These messages have been used of God to the conversion of thousands to Christian burial and the rewriting of their wills, in Canada, the United States, and other lands. Such information has been received by the author, unsolicited.

It has been pointed out that Christians could do a real service for God and His people by placing a copy of *Cremation—Is It Christian?* in every Christian home of their acquaintance. Large sums of money are being spent to revive this ancient, heathen custom in an effort to persuade the uninformed that cremation is a modern and dignified method of disposal.

This revised and enlarged pamphlet is sent forth with the prayer that God will continue to bless its ministry to all who sincerely desire to live and be laid away in accordance with the will of God.

The Author

FOREWORD

God did not choose to have all His revelations recorded in Scripture, but therein and in universal anthropological evidences the student of Biblical theology finds abundant evidence to reconstruct practices which could not conceivably have arisen independently in all parts of the world; they must have had some common authoritative source. God must have revealed to Adam and Eve the acceptable and appropriate method of returning "dust to dust." The modern archaeologist in almost every land takes careful note of the position of burial, the dress, the artifacts put in the grave with the body and any indications of anticipated life after death.

From earliest indications, burial has been the public testimony of assurance of physical resurrection. Can you imagine that God would appoint cremation in anticipation of raising His only begotten Son from the dead! He was known as the God of Abraham, Isaac, and Jacob—the God of the living. Even more than among many Christians today, Hebrew believers kept separate references to the body and references to the person who had once inhabited the body, for to be absent from the body is to be present with the Lord.

This was the public declaration of Job from the midst of great testing. Worms—not fire—would destroy his body, yet in that same body (resurrected) he would behold his Redeemer (Job 19:25-27). This is the testimony of every believer who pictures publicly his union with the Lord in death, burial, and resurrection through believer's baptism (Romans 6:4). Can you imagine that God would have permitted cremation when public burial in water was so closely knit in the message of the new Church, "Believe and be baptized!"

The word for sanctification means, basically, set apart

unto God. The author of these studies argues for burial in consecrated ground, that set aside in dedication unto God and respected thereafter. This dedication likewise expresses our hope that in Christ shall all be made alive. Let any Christian look carefully at the teachings of Scripture, as set forth here by the Rev. James W. Fraser, before examining the commercial arguments of modern paganism.

Warren Vanhetloo
Central Conservative Baptist Theological Seminary
Minneapolis, Minnesota

THE SUPREME CURSE

In the law of God it was decreed
That Israel's land be purged and freed
Of images, idols, statues, and groves
By burning to ash, tho' hidden in coves.
They were cremated in public view
At God's command, both old and new.

When Achan saw that wedge of gold
And costly garment he could neatly fold,
With shekels of silver, all shining and new,
He decided at once to carry through
A secret plan that none would know,
Thus help to make his fortunes grow.

He confessed his sin, but 'twas too late;
He could not re-enter mercy's gate.
He was stoned with stones until he died
For appearing as if he had never lied.
They laid him upon a new-built pyre
And reduced him to ashes in the angry fire.

For heathen gods and certain crimes
Was death and cremation—there were no fines.
This was God's curse and immediate sentence,
Regardless of confession or deep repentance:
Swept from the earth by a purging fire,
And reduced to ashes upon a pyre.

Moses then burnt their golden calf
And reduced their god to bitter chaff;
David and his men burnt Philistine gods
And spread their ash upon the clods.
Jehu, too, burnt their gods of Baal,
Not even putting them up for sale.

Shall we, in this enlightened age,
Refuse to obey the sacred page;
Treating our dead as if divinely cursed,
In crematory fires wholly immersed?
Dear fellow Christian, be warned in time,
Don't burn your friends in fire or lime!

J. W. Fraser

IS CREMATION CHRISTIAN?

> Know ye not that your body is the temple of
> the Holy Ghost which is in you, which ye have
> of God, and ye are not your own? For ye are
> bought with a price: therefore glorify God in
> your body, and in your spirit, which are God's
> (1 Corinthians 6:19-20).

One of the great Bible doctrines which has almost been forgotten in the last few years is the sanctity of the Christian's body. This text plainly states that our bodies are not our own to do with as we please. They belong to God because of creation and redemption. They are holy because they are cleansed and sanctified by the blood of Christ. They are also temples of the Holy Spirit and members of the body of Christ. These and many other Bible statements clearly set forth the truth of the divine ownership and sanctity of the Christian's body.

In dealing with this question of cremation we must not ignore the positive statements of Scripture if we would sincerely seek the Christian position on this issue. We know that in many localities a question of this kind is of little importance. In places far from large cities the question of cremation is seldom, if ever, raised; but in thickly populated areas this is not the case. When a relative passes on, the question comes up: shall it be cremation or burial? Questions have been asked by intelligent people: Is it wrong for a Christian's body to be cremated? Is it true that the body comes to life in the process of cremation? Recently, I was asked, "Why is cremation unpopular in Christian lands?"

I frankly admit I have not the last word on these questions, but confess I have given serious and prolonged thought to the question of Christian burial. What I may say

is not the result of an overnight meditation or snap judgment. This sermon has been called forth as a result of questions put to me by sincere people and also because of
doubts and questions in my own mind over a period of
years. I am giving what I have gleaned in the hope that
others will find the answers to their questions on this subject.

By the grace of God I have served as a minister of the
gospel since 1921. I had never been requested to officiate at
the funeral service of a body that was to be cremated until
I came to Montreal. To date, I have taken but one cremation service; what was very disturbing to me in that in-
stance was the fact that the individual had been a baptist. I
had not been notified that it was to be a cremation until I
arrived at the chapel at the hour of service. That service
was for me a conscience-stirring experience.

This event caused me deep concern as to my personal
responsibility as a minister of the gospel and as a leader
among Christian people of this generation. For I sincerely
believe that the minister's responsibility to God and to his
fellows is much greater than that of the average Christian.
We know all Christians are stewards of God and will be
called to account for their stewardship in a coming day,
but preachers are especially honored and privileged ser-
vants; therefore, their responsibility is greater.

This new experience caused me to study again the whole
question of Christian burial. I searched the Scriptures on
this subject with greater avidity than I had done hereto-
fore. In my quest I made the discovery that very few, if any,
articles have been written or sermons preached by the
clergy, either for cremation or against it. So as I proceed to
state my findings, I trust you will follow me with an open
mind.

According to *Webster's Unabridged Dictionary,* the word
"cremation" is from the Latin *crematio,* from *cremo,* which
means "to burn—burning, particularly the burning of the
dead according to the customs of many ancient nations."

The *Encyclopaedia Britannica* states that "cremation is
the burning of human corpus which was the general practice of the ancient world, with the important exceptions of
Egypt, where bodies were embalmed; Judea (or Ancient

Israel) where they were buried in sepulchres, and China, where they were buried in the earth. Cremation is still practiced over a great part of Asia and America, but not always in the same form. Thus the ashes may be stored in urns, or buried in the earth, or thrown to the wind, or, as among the Digger Indians, smeared with gum on the heads of the mourners."

Our modern crematories are specially constructed buildings erected for the purpose of the incineration of human bodies, having individual compartments which are heated to a temperature that quickly reduces the body to ashes. The usual committal service is held in the crematory chapel, after which the friends leave. The casket is then placed in one of the compartments, the shape of an oversized coffin, at which point the cremation process commences. When the heat becomes intense, the body appears to be very much alive as it jumps about, which is the result of the contraction and expansion of the muscles.

To me it is a rather gruesome and unkind thing to do to the body of a loved one. Can you imagine yourself being responsible for the cremation of the body of your mother, your husband, your wife, or your child? To a person of refined Christian culture, it must be most repulsive to think of the body of a friend being treated like a beef roast in an oven, with all its running fats and sizzling tissues.

The body is reduced to ashes in a white heat of 2,000° F. in a few hours. In the more recently built crematories, it is claimed that this is done in less than one hour. When cooled, the ashes are put into an urn. The remains of a body weighing about 140 pounds would be no more than three to four pounds of ash.

Were it not for the Christian's responsibility to God, there is something that can be said in favor of cremation. It may be less expensive than burial, because a cemetery lot is unnecessary, although some do bury the ashes. The laws of Canada and some other lands do not compel you to bury the ashes: you may throw them to the winds, or cast them into the sea; you are at liberty to dispose of them in almost any way you please; you may bury them in your lawn or back yard, or divide them equally among the family, or keep them in your pantry.

If people only knew their Bible, I am sure they would be more careful with the remains of their loved ones. According to divine standards, it was a supreme dishonor and curse for a person to have no burial. Such a curse was pronounced by God on King Jehoiakim of Jerusalem because of his pride and disobedience to God. The prophet Jeremiah said of him, "He shall be buried with the burial of an ass" (Jeremiah 22:19); which meant, he shall have no burial at all. Josephus, the Jewish historian, states that Jehoiakim's body was cast out by the king of Babylon, and lay exposed and unburied some distance from the gate of Jerusalem. There are a number in the Bible who were thus cursed for their disobedience to God: Achan (Joshua 7:15); Jezebel (2 Kings 9:30-37); Ahab's offspring (1 Kings 21:17-24); Sisera and Jabin (Psalm 83:9-10); and others. If we dishonor friends by cremation we shall be called to account for it (Romans 14:12; 2 Corinthians 5:10).

Another "advantage" of cremation is that if you wish to bury the remains in another land, the freight charges are small, or you can carry them with your luggage; and then, too, a second undertaker is not necessary.

When we mention the transportation of the dead from one place to another, I think of the case of the patriarch, Joseph. He died in Egypt but did not wish his remains to stay there; so, previous to his decease, he took an oath of his people, saying, "God will surely visit you, and ye shall carry up my bones from hence." He died at the age of 110 years; they embalmed him and put him in a coffin (Genesis 50:24-26).

About 300 years later his people left Egypt to go to the promised land. In Exodus 13:19 we read, "And Moses took up the bones of Joseph with him." His people carried his remains in the coffin all through that long, long journey. And then in Joshua 24:32, which was about forty years later, we read, "And the bones of Joseph, which the children of Israel brought up out of Egypt, buried they in Shechem, in a parcel of ground which Jacob bought ... and it became the inheritance of the children of Joseph [Israel]."

If Moses had cremated the body of Joseph before commencing that long journey, the question of transportation would have been much simpler. Instead of carrying that costly, bulky, Egyptian coffin with its contents, one of the grandsons could have carried the urn with his household baggage. But no! This heathen custom of cremation must not be practiced among God's people. For them, there was only one way to dispose of their dead and that was by the sacred custom of burial.

A large and important place is given in the Bible to the burial of the faithful. The whole of Genesis 23 is devoted to recording the death and burial of Sarah, Abraham's wife. The sacred writer devoted almost one half of Genesis 50 to the record of Jacob's death and burial. There are some to-day who assert that it doesn't matter how our bodies are disposed of. Such an attitude betrays a poor knowledge of the letter and the spirit of the Word of God. Why did God bury Moses? He could have disposed of his body in many other ways (Deuteronomy 34:5-8). Burial is the only God-given way of honorably disposing of the dead.

Bear in mind, beloved, that this sermon is preached only for the benefit of those who sincerely fear and worship God and who accept the Bible as final and adequate in all matters of doctrine and conduct.

Now let me quote another Bible incident which gives us to understand what God thinks about the burning of human bodies. In Amos 2:1 we have the record of Moab's unpardonable sin. Remember that Moab was considered a heathen nation. This account serves to prove that God takes notice of the doings of the most ungodly. Let me quote the verse: "Thus saith the LORD: For three transgressions of Moab, and for four, I will not turn away the punishment thereof; because he burned the bones of the king of Edom into lime." If there is any verse in the Bible that positively emphasizes God's disapproval of the burning of human bodies, it is this. God plagued and punished Moab for this immoral and unpardoned sin.

I wish to briefly state at least four reasons why, as a Christian, I cannot lend my support to the practice of cremation.

First of All, Because It Is of Heathen Origin

It is not difficult to understand why people who are not well acquainted with the Holy Scriptures lend their support to this pagan practice. I was not surprised when I read in the *Montreal Star* in 1953 that Joseph Stalin requested that his body be cremated. He was not a Christian but a communist, and naturally would not have a conscience about it. However, contrary to his request, his body was actually embalmed and, years later, buried (on November 1, 1961).

Then, too, let us mention another communist, the late Andrei Y. Vishinsky, the chief Soviet delegate to the United Nations. He died of a heart attack on November 22, 1954, at the age of 71 years, in New York. His body was laid in a copper-lined casket which cost $8,000 and was flown to Moscow by way of France. He lay in state for a time in Moscow's historic Hall of Columns, after which his body was cremated. Communism has done everything possible to obliterate the standards and customs of Christianity, even to that of Christian burial.

According to historical records, the idea of reducing human bodies to ashes originated in ancient heathen lands. Rome was among the first to practice this abhorrent custom. Today, in India, this is a common practice among the Hindus, but the Muhammadans bury their dead.

I asked a missionary from India if the Christians of that land cremated their dead. With a look of surprise he said, "Positively not! Cremation is heathen. The Christians of India bury their dead, because burial is Christian." There is absolutely nothing Christian about cremation; it is as pagan as idol worship.

In the year 1873 a physician, Sir Henry Thompson, advocated the introduction of cremation into England on the basis of sanitation. But strong public feeling was against the innovation, with the result that it has made very little progress. The first crematory built in the United States was in Washington, Pennsylvania, in 1876. It was first used for the incineration of the body of Baron DePalm in December of that year. Some have requested cremation in an attempt to escape the resurrection and the life to come. How utterly ignorant and foolish of them.

According to the *Reader's Digest* of January 1964, the percentage of cremations to burials has stayed at less than 4 percent in the United States during the last ten years. But regardless of how popular or unpopular this practice is or may become, it is still pagan.

Secondly, Because It Is an Aid to Crime

This is something that is not very well known but is one of the reasons why the practice has made little headway in Christian lands. It has been stated by those who are in a position to know, that, in the detection of criminal poisoning, a proper analysis cannot be obtained after cremation; therefore, it is a positive aid to crime. There should be a law in our land forbidding the cremation of all bodies having died from poisoning or other suspicious causes. I am pleased, however, to learn that the "Acts of Burial" for the Province of Quebec states: "No burial (or cremation) can take place before the expiration of twenty-four hours after decease, unless special permission has been obtained from the police."

The sudden death of a certain man in an eastern Ontario city attracted much public attention. After the burial a common rumor resulted in a postmortem examination, which yielded evidence that the deceased had died as a result of a dose of strychnine. An arrest was made and, after questioning, the accused was committed to trial for murder by judge and jury but was acquitted because of insufficient evidence. We were told that it was one of those cases where they knew who was responsible but could not at the time secure sufficient legal evidence. But this is why I refer to the incident: Before the arrest, the accused said to a certain mortician, "My mistake was that I did not have his body cremated." Every person with a Christian conscience should avoid even thinking favorably of this screen to crime.

Thirdly, Because It Is a Barbarous Act

Here is an extract from a letter from a British Columbia reader to the *Sunday School Times* of September 1934: "The question of cremation was brought home to us when our mother was called Home. At first it was decided to cremate her body, principally with the thought of some day taking her 'ashes' to the old home in the East and bury-ing them in the family plot in the old cemetery. On finding out the process of cremation, from first to last, we im-mediately decided in favor of burial. Anyone who knows little or nothing about cremation should find out all about it before cremating the body of a loved one. Even from a human standpoint, without considering the religious side of the question, it seems wrong."

A great many refined people shrink from consigning the bodies of loved ones to destruction by the process of cremation because of its apparent inhuman and pagan aspect. After all, the custom was handed down from the barbarous people of the Dark Ages. Most certainly it is in-human and godless, to say the least.

I am not concerned about the resurrection of bodies that have been cremated, for God can, and He will, raise from the dead all bodies of believers and unbelievers who have been burned, buried, or eaten, and all who lie in the depths of the seas, or who have been blown to atoms, or destroyed in any way, for His power and ability are infinite.

When we lay away the body in the grave, according to the sentence of God, it returns to earth in the natural way or by an act of God, whereas cremation is an act of man. God said, "Out of it [the ground] wast thou taken: for dust thou art, and unto dust shalt thou return" (Genesis 3:19). According to divine precept and example there is but one Christian way to dispose of our dead and that is to bury them. This brings me to my last, but most important, point.

Fourthly, Because Cremation Is Anti-Biblical, Therefore, Unchristian

One of the most elementary principles of Christian thought and life is expressed in the apostolic words, "Ye are not your own" (1 Corinthians 6:19). This sense of divine ownership, rather than self-ownership, is the inspiration of all Christian dignity and strength. The doctrine of the resurrection reminds us that the body is not to be treated as a temporary thing, as belonging to this stage of ex-istence only.

Rather than give our consent to destroy God's property

in the oven of a crematory, every loved one should be affectionately and carefully laid away whole in the mother earth, like the body of our Saviour. His body was lovingly and tenderly prepared for burial according to the customs of God's people (John 19:38-42). The Hebrew people considered as sacred all burial grounds and marked the place where each body was interred.

Perhaps one reason why some Christians have had their friends' bodies cremated is that many preachers have failed to teach the great Bible doctrine of the sanctity of the Christian's body. Many, who claim to have declared the whole council of God, have never taught or preached this major subject. This is a very grave omission, for in Malachi 2:7 we read, "For the [preacher's] lips should keep knowledge, and they [the people] should seek the law at his mouth; for he is the messenger of the Lord."

The sanctity of the body was a doctrine in Israel that was carefully taught. They were charged that they must not copy the customs of the heathen nations. They were expressly taught not to cut, mark, or tattoo their bodies (Deuteronomy 14:1-2). This teaching of the sacredness of the bodies of God's people is carried into the New Testament and is enjoined upon Christians everywhere in such portions as 1 Corinthians 6:9-20; Romans 6:13; 12:1. In Romans 14:8 the apostle says, "Whether we live therefore, or die, we are the Lord's." Christianity not only concerns itself with the soul but also with the body, for both have been redeemed.

The Apostle Paul, like his Saviour, often taught great lessons by asking questions and then answering them. In 1 Corinthians 6:9-20 he asks four questions as he proceeds to prove the sacredness of the Christian's body. Just briefly I will mention three:

"Know ye not that the unrighteous shall not inherit the kingdom of God?" Then in verses 9 and 10 he names ten classes of society which are disqualified for Heaven. These Corinthians were heathen when Paul first preached the gospel to them. They had been a wicked and unclean people, but by acknowledging to God their guilt and accepting Christ as their Saviour, they became children of God. Then Paul asks another question:

"Know ye not that your bodies are the members of Christ?" He goes on to say, "Shall I then take the members of Christ and use them for immoral purposes?" He then makes this observation, "He that is joined unto the Lord is one spirit." He is proving the oneness of the believer with his Lord. In the light of this statement it is an immoral act to abuse the body by subjecting it to cremation.

"What? know ye not that your body is the temple of the Holy Ghost which is in you, which ye have of God, and ye are not your own? For ye are bought with a price: therefore glorify God in your body, and in your spirit, which are God's" (verses 19-20).

Now, then, we have observed that the Holy Scriptures teach that:

The Christian way of disposing of our dead is by burial only, as exemplified in sacred history.

God does not approve of the burning of human bodies—even of our enemies. This was one of Moab's unpardoned sins (Amos 2:1).

Our bodies are the members of Christ (1 Corinthians 6:15).

Our bodies are the temples of the Holy Ghost (1 Corinthians 6:19).

Dead or alive our bodies belong to God because of redemption and sanctification (Romans 8:23; Hebrews 10:10).

Our bodies are the seed of the resurrection bodies (1 Corinthians 15:38).

Self-ownership is a pagan concept, and we are not free to do with our bodies as we please, if we would live in the will of God (1 Corinthians 6:20).

Cremation has come to us from the uncivilized, uncultured, pagan peoples of the Dark Ages . . . those whose minds were distorted by sin, of whom Plato said, "Man has sunk below the beast of the brutes" . . . people who bored out the eyes of their fellows, tore out their tongues by the roots, burned them alive, and also fed them to the lions . . . people who practiced many other methods of fiendish cruelty. And yet, in these days of boasted, civilized culture and Christian refinement, some are still following this primitive fell custom of burning the bodies of their friends. This custom is positively unrefined, unholy, and pagan.

When asked recently to officiate at the funeral service of a body that was to be cremated, I sympathetically refused. When asked why, I replied, "As a minister of Jesus Christ I officiate only at Christian burials."

In answer to the question, "Is cremation Christian?" my answer is, "Positively no! It is of heathen origin, an aid to crime, a barbarous act, also anti-Biblical; therefore, *unchristian!*"

CREMATION IN THE BIBLE

> The graven images of their gods shall ye burn with fire (Deuteronomy 7:25).
> He that is taken with the accursed thing shall be burnt with fire, he and all that he hath (Joshua 7:15).

After giving my first message over the radio against the practice of cremating our Christian dead, I received a large number of letters from correspondents in all walks of life, in which were liberal expressions of appreciation for help received. I had expected to receive some letters approving of this primitive practice, but not even so much as one correspondent objected to my position in relation to this subject.

No doubt it is due to the fact that there cannot be found in the early writings and practices of the Christian Church one writer or leader who supported the heathen custom. Also, there is not to be found in the Holy Scriptures one sentence that even sympathizes with such an unholy practice as cremating the Christian dead. Down through the years Christians have shunned and disapproved of this uncultured practice. It was in the year 1886 that the Roman Catholic Church officially banned this gruesome practice. Long before that date, however, baptist pastors and their congregations spoke against and abhorred the pagan rite. Not only these but any group of people who accept the Bible as the Word of God and as their criterion for faith and practice can only condemn this heathen way of disposing of a Christian's body.

So, our stand against this barbarous practice is certainly not a new Christian attitude. It is a position that is easily supported by the Scriptures—that is, among those who accept the Holy Bible as adequate and final on all questions of religion and moral conduct. Against the sacred Scriptures there is no court of appeal, for they are settled and accepted in Heaven (Psalm 119:89). This question of cremation is not even debatable, for God has spoken the final word.

I am aware that there are some professing Christians even today who are semipagan in their concepts of life, who do not accept the Scriptures as sufficient in such a matter as the disposal of a redeemed body. They have practically forsaken divine revelation; from a position of human reasoning they have interjected their own compromising interpretations on the subject and have fallen prey to the ancient, heathen custom. However, I will endeavor to state four further reasons why the cremating of the human body is anti-Christian.

I have chosen these texts (Deuteronomy 7:25 and Joshua 7:15) to show that cremation was, in God's sight, the most dishonorable of all disposals. When God commanded it, it was in severe punishment of an unworthy individual or of the abominable idols of the heathen. Whenever the gods of the heathen nations fell into the hands of the Israelites, they were to be reduced to ashes immediately. This was the law of God (Deuteronomy 7:5, 25), and we see how it was obeyed by David and his men in 1 Chronicles 14:12 and by Jehu in 2 Kings 10:26.

Also, during the life of Moses we have an incident recorded in Exodus 32:1-24 as to how this was done. When he went up into the mountain to receive the tables of the law, he was absent from the people of Israel for forty days. They became restless and, like the Egyptians, wanted a god they could see. They brought their gold trinkets to Aaron, and of them he made a calf. The calf was one of the prominent gods of Egypt at that time. When Moses came down out of the mount he saw the golden calf and the people dancing about it. He made the sad discovery that they had fallen into idolatry. He took their god and burned it in the fire and ground it to dust. Why did he burn it? Because this was God's sentence against all such abominable idols. Does it seem right, therefore, that the body of a Christian friend should be treated like that of a heathen idol?

Then, too, in Joshua 7 we have the sad record of Achan's sin against God, his people, and himself. In this incident, we are given to see that cremation was to be the disposal of the accursed and unforgiven! A person's body ordered cremated was the divine sentence for wrongdoing! To be burned instead of buried was only for the person who had been guilty of special, aggravated sin. It was God's curse upon Achan. In our previous message we pointed out that, according to divine law, it was a supreme dishonor for a person to have no burial. It was so in the case of Achan, because he disgraced himself and his family by disobeying the command of God. He was cremated as part of the divine punishment for his sin. It was a harsh sentence, but Achan had troubled his own household and nation and was the cause of the death of thirty-six soldiers in Israel.

Since this is the picture as found in the Bible, do you think it proper to have the body of a Christian friend disposed of in this way? Would you wish to have your remains disgraced in this retributive, abhorrent manner? In the Bible such treatment was reserved for deliberate disobedience to the command of God.

Now then, I must proceed to mention my four further reasons why a refined, Bible-enlightened Christian cannot endorse or request in his will that his body be cremated.

Cremation Is Contrary to the Example and Teachings of Jesus and of the Apostolic Church

If only Christian people were better acquainted with the Bible, they would not do such a dishonor to their deceased friends. From any angle you may look at this subject, the fact remains that an honest soul who is familiar with the Bible will confess that cremation does not belong to a refined Christian culture, nor is it the request of one who has surrendered soul and body to Jesus Christ. We do not take issue with non-Christians in this matter. If they do not accept the Bible as God's Word, in reality they have no criterion by which to judge right and wrong. Their own thoughts and personal views are to them supreme. It is a most foolish and dangerous attitude toward life, we know. In fact, King Solomon said under divine inspiration, "He that trusteth in his own heart is a fool" (Proverbs 28:26). This deceitful attitude of setting aside or rejecting the Bible and its message is a foolish philosophy, to say the least. It is like a man going to sea without a chart or compass, like climbing a mountain without a guide or equipment, like a student without a teacher or textbook. An unbeliever has no supernatural guide or spiritual understanding that would enable him to make the right and proper choice.

One of the great disadvantages of this generation is a limited or partial knowledge of only certain parts of the Bible. This has given rise to many false statements by those who claim to know it. Recently, I read of a certain religious leader who said, "There is nothing in the Holy Scriptures that forbids cremation." Whoever he was, I think he would do society a kindness if he would carefully re-read the sacred Book. There is certainly sufficient to show that cremation was held in disfavor and was associated with the abominable and cursed! To reason that there is nothing in Scripture which directly forbids the cremation of Christian bodies reveals a shallow mental attitude of compromise toward that which God abhors.

However, for the Christian, Jesus Christ is our example in life and in death, and that should be sufficient. But can you imagine a sincere person claiming to be a Christian and yet refusing to follow the example of Christ? Such an attitude is paradoxical and a direct contradiction of his profession!

The burial of Jesus was not coincident or accident, for previously the bodies of godly men and women were disposed of in that way. Burial was God's only method of disposal of the bodies of His people. Jesus Christ was buried, because burial was in harmony with the purposes of God (Isaiah 53:9). Burial is the only Christian method and scriptural disposal of a believer's remains.

As previously mentioned, in 1886 the Roman Catholic Church banned the practice of cremation for her priests and people for at least two very good reasons. First of all, historically cremation has been associated with the efforts of unbelievers in their denial of the resurrection of the body. The disposal of the body by cremation has, in recent years, been largely the choice of unbelievers and notorious characters. It is true that some good-living people have requested it, but you will agree that the vast majority have been questionable characters. Such men as Josef Stalin requested cremation, although in his case it was not carried out. Adolf Hitler, Andrei Y. Vishinsky, Adolf Eichmann, and nearly all of the notorious criminals of our day have also made that same request. There is a great deal of evidence that cremation is not usually the choice of the scripturally enlightened or moral-living individual.

It is folly of the most puerile kind to entertain the thought that by cremation one will escape the resurrection of the last day. However, since cremation largely is the choice of the unbelieving and ungodly, that alone is enough to cause refined Christian people to refuse to be partakers with them in this supposed attempt to escape the judgment.

Another reason why the Roman Catholic Church banned its practice was because it shows an irreverence for the body as a temple of the Holy Spirit. This, too, should be sufficient reason for any intelligent Christian to reject openly this ungodly pagan practice.

The Greek Orthodox Church does not favor cremation either. A discussion was touched off in the United States in 1961 by the cremation of the famed conductor, Dimitri Mitropoulous, a member of this church. Archbishop Iakovos, head of the Greek Orthodox Church in America, asked the ecumenical patriarch of Constantinople for a clarification of the Orthodox attitude toward cremation. The patriarch responded by saying, "There is no formal Orthodox rule against cremation, but there is a heavy weight of custom and sentiment in favor of Christian burial."

There is very little that can be said or written in favor of cremation. Even that which has been said by the International Cremation Federation is weak. In the federation's resolution passed at their three-day congress in Stockholm, Sweden, in May 1961, which was attended by 120 delegates representing fifteen countries, they recommended disposal by cremation on the grounds that it was aesthetic, sanitary, and economical.

Christian conviction compels me to point out that their

resolution contains a mixture of truth and error. To those who know nothing about the ugly truth of cremation, this may sound rather pacifying. I do agree that it is economical. It is the cheapest legal disposal of a human body that I know of in this land. But to say it is aesthetic could sound like the truth only to those who know nothing of the unpleasant and grotesque process of cremation. There is really nothing beautiful or graceful about any process of the disposal of a body but this is definitely less so when we revert to this modernized, heathen custom. How can one, who knows of the twitching and jumping and noises that there are when the heat is turned on to 2,000° F., look upon the process as aesthetic? It is anything but aesthetic. It is most revolting and repulsive to think of the body of a refined Christian being burned to a crisp and finally to ashes. There is absolutely nothing beautiful or graceful about it.

Some argue that it is sanitary—well, of course, so is burial. But then, this is why, in the larger-populated areas, they gather and burn the refuse and garbage of our cities. Does a human body that has served God, that has been purchased by a divine price (1 Corinthians 6:15, 20), that has been indwelt by the Holy Spirit (1 Corinthians 6:19), and served its generation in the will of God, deserve this kind of uncultured treatment? Because of the example of Christ, the claims of God, and the divine ownership of body and soul, there is a sanctity to the believer's body that the average individual has not realized. If he did, no Christian would ever will that his body be destroyed by the fire of a crematory. Then, too, a Christian objects to cremation because:

Cremation Is a Supreme Dishonor to a Redeemed Body

> "Ye are not your own. For ye are bought
> with a price: therefore glorify God in your
> *body,* and in your spirit, which are God's"
> (1 Corinthians 6:19-20).

The body of every Christian belongs not to himself but to God in the very same sense in which the spirit or soul belongs to Him. Therefore, to subject that which belongs to God to an immoral, heathen custom is sin! This body of flesh and blood, as well as the resurrection body to be, equally belong to God, because of redemption.

Ethnologists have listed about thirty methods of disposing of the human body, but there is only one honorable way of disposing of a Christian's body—and that is burial. I have yet to meet or read of a recognized Bible teacher who teaches that cremation is Christian. I know there is a small class of professed Christians who actually think it brave and smart to violate the customs and laws of Christian society. They have asked that their ashes be strewn along a railroad track, or scattered on a river, lake, or at sea, and others that their ashes be cast to the winds anywhere—anywhere rather than have them deposited in consecrated ground. Such requests and decisions indicate an unspiritual character. There seems to be a strong desire by such a class to break away from the teaching and example of Christ and His apostles.

We have already stated that cremation is a pagan custom which has come down to us from the uncivilized, uncultured, heathen people of the Dark Ages. Long before the time of Christ it was an accepted practice of the backward, primitive, superstitious tribes and nations. It was a custom of the Gentile nations surrounding Israel at the time of Christ and His apostles. Neither He nor they ever looked upon it with approval, either by precept or example. To Jesus Christ and the early Church, cremation was one of the abominations of the godless and unenlightened peoples. For Christians in this age of learning to adopt such an unholy custom is the equivalent of taking a long step backward to the uncouth and primitive customs of the unlearned of the superstitious ages.

No man of any academic standing can find one sentence of Scripture to support the burning of the bodies of honorable Christian people. When I preached and published my first sermon against cremation, I expected a letter or two of protest but was surprised, for not one was received. But I have received literally thousands in commendation and also telling of the changing of wills from cremation to Christian burial. These were unsolicited. I haven't room in this brief message to insert excerpts from letters of some of Canada's and the United States' distinguished citizens. The reason for such a response is that every intelligent Christian knows that Jesus and the apostolate in spirit and example witnessed against such a sacrilegious act.

Cremation Destroys the Sacred Memory of Our Beloved Dead

The Bible states that one of the degenerate evils of the last days is the absence of natural affection in family and social life—"without natural affection" (2 Timothy 3:3). In no other manner is this lack of affection being exhibited so forcefully as by the many who have friends cremated!

A friend of mine, who visited a crematory, noticed a pile of urns stacked one upon another. He asked the attendant if they were his stock of empties. Reluctantly he said, "They contain the ashes of bodies that have been cremated, but the relatives never thought enough of them to return and claim them." What a cheap way of unloading a sacred responsibility, isn't it? It is also a quick way of destroying the memory of the deceased.

Where there is a sacred respect for the deceased, it is evidenced by a reverent committal and a marking and a protecting of the place of interment. But usually, following the average cremation, there are no markers, tombstones, or monuments erected to one's memory. I believe it to be a most cruel and dishonoring act against the memory of the dead. Usually there is no grave to visit and decorate; no sacred spot where the remains of a friend lie. It is a demoralizing practice when you think of it in this way. It is a cruel way of desecrating the memory of a loved one, isn't it?

When the devoted wife of a certain citizen passed away, the husband had her body cremated. He was loath to part with even her ashes. For years he kept the urn in the home with an expensive wreath over it. It was really not the proper thing to do. However, after awhile, the daughter became tired of having it in the home, so she had it buried in the backyard. The following year the property was sold;

the family moved out and left the sacred remains of the mother in an unmarked spot in unconsecrated ground. How unintentionally cruel! The circumstances produced an unholy disrespect for the sacred remains of a devoted mother. Do you think that was a Christian thing to do?

I have been informed, by one who was in a position to know, that the remains of a certain family who had been cremated were finally put out with the local garbage and carried to the dump. How repulsive this is, even to tell of it! What a brutal dishonor done to those loved ones! There are similar incidents that could be repeated, but I must refrain. I just wish to emphasize that cremation is one of the quickest ways of destroying the sacred memory of the deceased!

Cremation Is the Cheapest Way of Discharging a Sacred Responsibility

There is no Biblical or Christian position that can favor cremation of an honorable believer's body, because it is wholly pagan and is nowhere favored by God nor practiced by the godly. There is no period in the early history of the Church when deceased believers were cremated.

In the time of the catacombs under the city of Rome, when the Church went underground because of bitter persecution, deceased believers were carefully laid away in the rock-hewn tombs, sealed and marked to identify them. If ever sanitary conditions would have excused cremation, it was then. But the abhorrent practice was never allowed, and, although the unbelieving Romans practiced it at that time, the Christians looked upon it with disfavor because it was an ungodly, heathen custom. It is estimated that about 3,000,000 believers were buried in those subterranean passages.

Usually, where there is warm affection, no man will dispose of a loved one, because the method is the cheapest. I think of Abraham, when Sarah died in those primitive times. He could have buried her somewhere in the wide open spaces, and it would have cost him nothing. But he didn't because he loved her, and, too, he was a God-fearing man. The whole of Genesis 23 is occupied with the death and burial of Sarah. There is a reason for this. Abraham never owned a foot of land, but, when his wife died, he bought a piece of land that would serve as a cemetery. He would not accept it as a gift; he paid 400 pieces of silver for it. To him, the laying away of his wife was a sacred matter. This became consecrated ground and was kept solely for the purpose of a cemetery. The three covenant fathers and their wives were later buried there.

There is a divine reason why all this account was written into the sacred Scriptures. "Whatsoever things were written aforetime were written for our learning" (Romans 15:4). It is not only folly but ignorance for one to argue that cremation is now Christian. It never can be while the whole spirit of Scripture is against it. Even if certain so-called Christian groups were to endorse it, that does not make it Christian. It is still a cruel, uncultured, pagan way of disposing of the dead.

It is true that the majority of cremated remains are never deposited in consecrated, marked, burial places. This is, to say the least, doing a supreme dishonor to the deceased's sacred remains.

In conclusion, let me recapitulate:

Cremation is contrary to the example and teachings of Jesus and of the apostolic Church.

Cremation does a supreme dishonor to a redeemed body.

Cremation destroys the sacred memory of our beloved dead.

Cremation is the cheapest legal way of discharging a sacred responsibility.

BARBARIANISM

A mother was kind and gentle and true,
Had three little angels; oh, how they grew;
With dimples and curls, and contagious smiles;
Were fat and chubby; at play they ran miles.
They were healthy and happy and winsome, too;
Were the loveliest darlings this mother knew.

This charmed mother was a willing slave.
Her three from disease she fought to save.
She toiled all day and nursed all night,
And put up for them a terrific fight.
Through the help of God and by her care,
He raised them up in answer to prayer.

With mother's help they grew mature;
Men and maiden were taught to be pure.
The three all married and moved away,
With the promise to return some better day.
Mother became lonely and rather poor.
She rented a room on a Rue Lefleur.

Her form was stooped, her face was drawn,
Her hair was gray and her children gone.
She fainted one day while on the street,
And could stand no more upon her feet.
That saintly mother, with a love so true,
Was left alone to battle through.

She was weak and sick with none to care,
Not even a friend to say a prayer.
But God's angels came and took her home,
That forsaken woman, so sad and lone.
This mother, who was once a willing slave,
Was denied the favor of an earthly grave.

The one-time dimpled and angelic three
Were now cold and cruel, as you will see;
For they ordered her body reduced to ashes—
The cheapest disposal, the burial of asses.
A pagan ordeal, so godless and cruel;
Don't treat *your mother* as you would a mule!

J. W. Fraser